30 Nonfiction Book Reports

by Deborah Rovin-Murphy

SCHOLASTIC
PROFESSIONAL BOOKS

New York • Toronto • London • Auckland • Sydney • Mexico City • New Delhi • Hong Kong • Buenos Aires

To Frank, for stepping on the writing path
with me so many years ago. Thank you.

Acknowledgments

For their time, energy and enthusiasm for project making
I gladly acknowledge and thank Joseph Donahue, Daniel Flor,
and Amelia Knipmeyer.

Cover design by Gerard Fuchs

Interior design by Ellen Matlach Hassell
for Boultinghouse & Boultinghouse, Inc.

Interior illustrations by Jason Robinson

ISBN: 0-439-37072-8

Copyright © 2003 by Deborah Rovin-Murphy

Published by Scholastic Inc.

Contents

ACTIVITIES

Introduction

Why Nonfiction?

Children are fascinated with the world around them. They gather facts, look at pictures, and write about topics of interest. Reading nonfiction is an important skill—students must be able to "read to learn." But, all too often, when children are asked to respond to the nonfiction they've read, they must present their facts in the same old way—the research report.

As adults, much of the information we gather comes to us via newspapers, articles, and essays. When we want to learn how to start a home repair project, plan a trip, handle finances, and even raise a child, we search for a book about it—a nonfiction book. Being able to locate the answers you are looking for, as well as synthesize and apply information to new situations, is a skill that children are never too young to try. Writing a report that lists facts and figures will not help a child to become excited about nonfiction. By using the creative projects in this book, children can challenge themselves to apply what they have learned and make decisions about the importance of certain parts of their topic.

The projects in this book give children the freedom to explore topics of interest in fresh and fun ways. They address different learning styles as well as foster creativity and critical thinking, helping students become actively engaged in their research.

Kids will become a primary resource in "Ask the Experts." They'll create an artifact in "Teaching Toys." They'll display their research in "Wear It Out!" And much more!

Getting Started

Use these introductory activities to pique students' interest in nonfiction. Ask students to think of a question that could be answered by research. Examples could be: *What animals live in the rainforest? What kinds of foods did people eat in ancient Rome?* Explain that, often, the way we find answers to the questions we have is by reading nonfiction. Because many children prefer to read stories about amazing places and fanciful characters in fiction books, encourage them to explore the genre of nonfiction by sharing interesting and unusual facts that may be found in nonfiction books. The activities in this book can be used throughout the year as the class studies different topics. They might also be the focus of an end of the year project in which students are evaluated on their research techniques and skills.

Create Interest

Ask students what they are curious about. Record students' ideas on chart paper.

Animals	Science	History
penguins	tornados	pyramids
dogs	butterflies	13 colonies
		knights
Sports	**People**	
soccer	presidents	

Scavenger Hunt

Introduce your students to the world of nonfiction with a factual scavenger hunt. First, look at the nonfiction titles you have in your classroom library. Select a range of titles across a variety of subject areas (history, science, how-to, biography, animals, math, and so on). Make up several simple questions about the topics of the books and display the books on the board. Read a question aloud and have students figure out what book would contain the answer. Next, divide the class into small groups. Each group gets a nonfiction book (place corresponding questions inside, on index cards) and tries to locate the answers to the questions. Rotate the books through each group until everyone has the answers to all of the questions.

Helping Students Select a Topic

Ask students what they would like to know more about, and have them come up with a research question (for instance, *What types of animals live in the desert? Why do people get viruses? How is peanut butter made?*). Encourage them to choose something that they are curious about. When helping a student select a book for research, keep in mind their interests and reading ability. Depending on their reading level, you might help students select a picture book, easy reader, or chapter book. Here are some possible research topics.

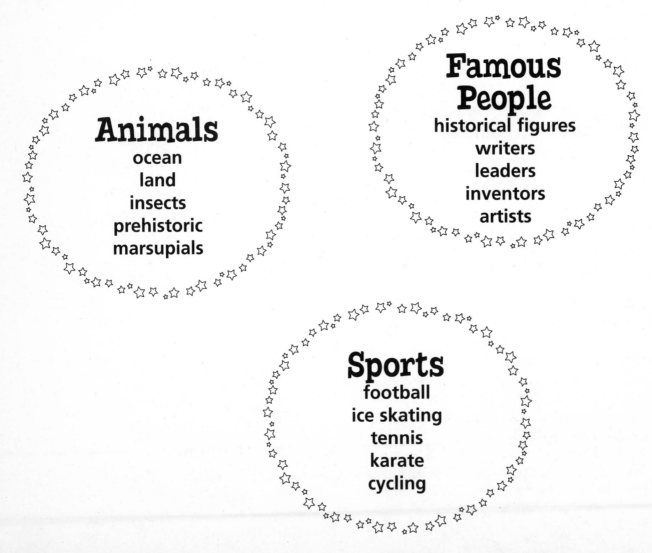

Animals
ocean
land
insects
prehistoric
marsupials

Famous People
historical figures
writers
leaders
inventors
artists

Sports
football
ice skating
tennis
karate
cycling

Geography
continents
countries
land forms
states
cartography

History
Middle Ages
exploration
Civil War
Industrial Revolution
Lewis and Clark

Science
electricity
the senses
matter
life cycles
simple machines

Nature
plants
weather
rainforests
pollution
ponds

Cultures
Japan
Mexico
Egypt
India
Navajo

Space
planets
sun
moon
stars
space travel

1 ABC Topic Books

Students organize factual information into an alphabet book format.

►Materials◄

- paper
- pencils
- markers
- crayons
- colored pencils

1 Have students write their topic at the top of a sheet of paper and the letters of the alphabet, A to Z, down the left side.

2 Invite students to think of a fact about their topic for each letter. They can play with words to make their facts fit. For instance, "E—Eucalyptus leaves are a staple of the koala's diet. F—Far away in Australia is where these cuddly creatures live."

3 Give each student 26 pages, one for each letter of the alphabet. (For smaller books, you may fold seven sheets of paper in half.) Using the information from their brainstorming sheets, have students write and illustrate each page. Bind the books together and have students read them to a kindergarten or first grade class.

2 Facts in the Mail

Students write letters to communicate information.

►Materials◄

- **reproducible 1**, page 36 (one per student)

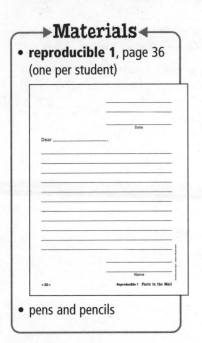

- pens and pencils

1 Share books such as *Postcards from Pluto* by Loreen Leedy (Holiday House, 1993) and *Your Best Friend, Kate* by Pat Brisson (Bradbury Press, 1989). These books are good examples of how to put factual information into letter format.

2 Ask students to think about the "where" in their research. Students may be researching a state, a time period, a habitat or environment, and so on. Invite them to imagine they are writing a letter home from one of these locations.

3 Remind students to incorporate facts by including them in their letters as observations. For instance, "I just stepped on the moon's surface with my new sneakers. My footprints will be here forever because there is no wind on the moon!" Have them write letters on their reproducibles, including their own personal touches. (For example, "Greetings from Ancient Egypt. I hope my writing doesn't look like hieroglyphics to you!")

12 Penny Lane
Anytown, U.S.A.
October 16
Date

Dear Mom and Dad,

The trees are tall here in the rain forest. I can see many colorful birds in the forest canopy.

My favorite animal is the howler monkey because he makes so much noise! My second favorite is the sloth because she sleeps so much.

Mom, you would not like it here. I saw a big snake! But you would like to see the beautiful orchids. Some smell like chocolate.

Your daughter,
Kama
Name

Reproducible 1 **Facts in the Mail**

►36◄

3 Read All About It!

Students write a newspaper article.

►Materials◄

- newspapers
- **reproducible 2**, page 37 (one per student)

- pens and pencils
- crayons or colored pencils

1 Discuss with students the six questions reporters ask when covering a story (*Who? What? When? Where? Why? How?*). Share local newspapers as examples of newspaper-style writing and features. Make a list of what they find on the board (headlines, advertisements, help wanted, comics, and so on).

2 Have students write down several interesting facts about their topic on a piece of blank paper. Next to each fact, students can write how they want to include that fact in their newspaper. Examples could be:

- The Tyrannosaurus Rex was a fierce dinosaur.
  Advertisement for T-Rex as a watchdog.
- Scientists who research dinosaurs are called Paleontologists.
  "Help Wanted" Ad.
- The Pteranodon was a dinosaur that could fly.
  Article.

3 Have students write and illustrate their stories.

4 Bind all pages into a class book, or display on a bulletin board.

4 Mini-Vocabulary Book

Students make a glossary of terms related to the topic.

►Materials◄
- drawing paper
- drawing supplies
- pens and pencils
- stapler

1 Tell students they will encounter topic-specific vocabulary words in their research. For examples of this, have students open up a social studies or science book and locate the glossary at the back of the book. Explain how knowing word meanings will help them better understand their topic. For example, a book about elections might include the vocabulary words *democrat, primary, ballot, electoral college,* and *representative*.

2 Have students list five vocabulary words specific to their research topic on one side of paper, and the definitions of the words on the other side.

3 To make the book, students fold a stack of paper in half and staple along the fold. They decorate the cover and put one or two vocabulary entries on each page.

4 Then students complete the mini-vocabulary book using their lists. Students should include pictures with the definition as well.

5 ▮ Travel Brochure

Students create a brochure to display facts.

►Materials◄
- oaktag
- drawing supplies

1 Show students samples of brochures from different countries, states, museums, historical places, and events. Explain that brochures are made to entice people to learn more about a certain place or topic.

2 Have students take the piece of oaktag and fold each edge toward the middle to make three sections.

3 First, have students create an eye-pleasing cover by making a catchy title such as "Soar to Saturn." Next, have students create a page with interesting facts. Then they can create a page that highlights a particular part of the area. Last, students can create a page using persuasive language and slogans such "Like the heat? Spend your next vacation on Mercury! "

4 Have students use photos, drawings, and diagrams to decorate their brochures. Display on a table or bulletin board.

6 Teaching Toys

Students create a toy that that represents their research topic.

►Materials◄

- paper
- pencils
- art supplies, such as construction paper, markers, paint, scissors, glue, clay, papier-mâché, cloth

1 Tell students that they will be making a museum gift shop display that will consist of toys representing their research topics.

2 Have students brainstorm a list of toys they see in museum gift shops (dolls, books, games, puzzles). Then have them pick an idea that would work with their specific topic. For instance, Dinosaurs—a clay model, Solar system—planet balls, George Washington—cut out doll.

3 Give each student a piece of blank construction paper so they may design or plan out what they are going to make. This will include a materials list, a diagram, and an explanation of how the toy that they are making will be a "teaching toy."

4 Students may present their toys to the whole class or in a small group. Extend learning by sorting the toys by object (doll, model, ball), category (history, science), or size. Place objects on display with a sign ("Our Class Museum Shop").

7 Ask the Experts

Students become expert authorities on their topics as they answer classmates' questions.

►Materials◄
- posterboard
- markers
- index cards
- pens or pencils

1 Make a class list on a large piece of posterboard. Write students' names down one side of the paper with the topic they are researching down the other.

2 Invite students to fill out index cards with questions to several "experts," write their name on the card, and leave the cards on the expert's desk. Some examples could be: *What types of food did the ancient Egyptians eat? Or How long did it take Alexander Graham Bell to invent the telephone?*

3 Each expert answers the question on the back of the index card and returns it to the inquiring student. If the expert does not know the answer to the question, encourage him or her to research further.

8 It's in the Bag!

Students gather artifacts related to their topics.

►Materials◄
- plain brown bags (one per student)
- glue
- art materials
- construction paper
- found objects

1 Have students decorate bags using art materials, pictures, or photos related to their topic.

2 Inside the bag, students place items (pictures, student-created or found objects) that relate to their topics. For instance, a student researching dinosaurs may include sand, a rock, a fossil, and pictures of dinosaurs.

3 Have students share the contents of their bags with the class explaining why they included each item. Display on a table with a sign, "Knowledge Is in the Bag!" Students can look in each others' bags to learn about different topics.

9 Magazine Covers

Students create the cover of a magazine that focuses on their topic.

▶Materials◀

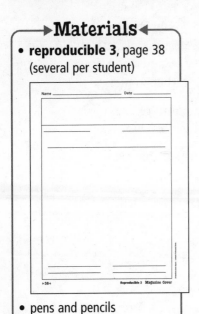

- **reproducible 3**, page 38 (several per student)
- pens and pencils
- drawing supplies

1 Show students various magazines that focus on a particular topic. Discuss with students the catchy names of the magazines as well as the attention-grabbing pictures and text on the covers.

2 Have students come up with a name for a magazine related to their topic. Next, have students use the smaller lines on the sides of the cover to create catchy article names. For instance, for the topic of ancient Egypt, the title might be *Hieroglyphics Weekly*, with an article called "10 Tips for Building a Lasting Pyramid."

3 As an extension, have students write one of the articles they've mentioned on their cover.

10 Getting Mathematical

Help students integrate math into their research.

→**Materials**←
- pens and pencils
- paper

1 Discuss with students the fact that math is connected to all of their research topics. Some examples are: the size of the planets, the life span of different animals, timelines, sport statistics, and so on. Invite students to generate five math-related facts related to their topics.

2 Students then use these facts as a starting point for math word problems. You might use the examples shown below.

3 Have students trade cards and solve each others' problems.

FACT: The Titanic sunk in 1912. Its location was discovered in 1985.

MATH PROBLEM: How long did it take for the Titanic to be discovered on the ocean floor?

FACT: Americans eat about 500,000,000 pounds of popcorn each year.

MATH PROBLEM: How much popcorn would be eaten in 5 years?

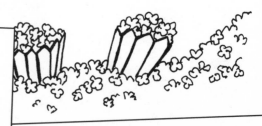

FACT: Insects have 6 legs, 3 body parts and 2 antennae.

MATH PROBLEM: There are 4 insects. How many legs, body parts, and antennae are there altogether?

11 Fun Fact Cards

Students create trading cards.

►Materials◄

- **reproducible 4**, page 39 (one per student)

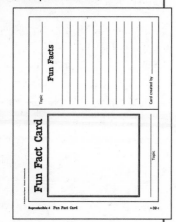

- construction paper
- glue
- drawing supplies
- pens and pencils

1 On their reproducibles, have students draw a picture or diagram that depicts their topic. They fill in the label underneath the picture with the name of the topic.

2 Have students write facts on the other half of the picture.

3 When the card is completed, students cut the sheet in half and mount back-to-back on colorful construction paper, then trim the paper around the card.

4 Students can have fun sharing their cards and trading with others. Store the finished cards in a large filing box for easy reference.

5 As an extension, play "Who Am I?" Give each child a card and have the other students ask yes or no questions, trying to determine the person's identity.

12 Made to Order

Students create a catalog page related to their topics.

►Materials◄

- **reproducible 5**, page 40 (one per student)

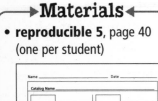

- drawing supplies
- pens and pencils

1 Bring in mail-order catalogs for students to look through for inspiration. Point out how items are shown and described.

2 Using the reproducible, have students choose six "products" related to their subject and write a short description.

3 Have students draw a picture of each product in the box provided. For instance, if the student is researching the Arctic, the items pictured might be ice blocks to build an igloo, sealskin clothing for protection from the cold, dogsled for traveling on the ice and snow, and Northern Lights postcards.

13 Compare It!

Students make a Venn diagram to compare and contrast information.

►Materials◄

- **reproducible 6**, page 41 (one per pair of students)

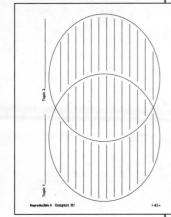

- pens and pencils

1 Draw a Venn diagram on the board. As an example, have students compare two topics they are familiar with (for instance, books and television).

2 Ask students to share information about the topics they are studying. List these topics on the board in categories such as time period, animals, biography, science, and so on.

3 Students with similar topics pair off and fill out the reproducible using information from their research. For instance, pairs might compare giraffes with koalas (animals), Roman times with Egyptian times (time periods), Wilma Rudolph with Abraham Lincoln (famous figures).

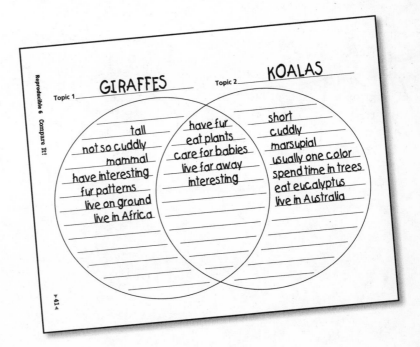

14 Hanging Out the Facts

Students create a classroom display of interesting facts.

▶Materials◀

- construction paper
- drawing supplies
- pens and pencils
- scissors
- clothesline
- clothespins
- basket

1 Have students write down five interesting facts about their topics. For example, *Theodore Roosevelt: He was the first president to fly in an airplane.*

2 Invite each student to draw and cut out pieces of construction paper to resemble pieces of clothing. Students write each of their facts on a separate piece of clothing. Hang clothesline with clothespins. Each week (or day) a student gets to "hang out" the interesting facts they have learned about their topic.

3 After all students have displayed their facts, put all clothes together and invite students to "sort" all the clothes into the right topic pile.

Sloths have black teeth.

Sloths live in rainforests.

Sloths sleep 18 hours a day.

Sloths are mammals.

Sloths have thick, wiry hair.

15 Documentaries

Students make and narrate a filmstrip about their topic.

►Materials◄

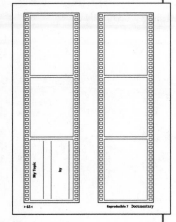

- cube-shaped tissue box (one per student)
- wrapping or construction paper
- drawing supplies
- **reproducible 7**, page 42 (one per student)
- tape

1 Have students cut the tops off tissue boxes. Then, wrap the box in wrapping or construction paper, leaving the cut side open.

2 Have students cut 3-inch slits opposite each other on two sides of the box, for pulling the filmstrip through.

3 On the reproducible, students draw five diagrams, illustrations, or maps. On a separate piece of paper, students number 1 to 5 and write a script to go along with each of the filmstrip panels.

4 Students cut out the filmstrips, tape them end to end, and pull them through the slits as they narrate their documentaries for the group.

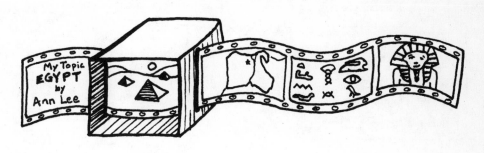

16 Just the Facts!

Students create a class encyclopedia of research topics.

►Materials◄

- looseleaf binder with dividers
- **reproducible 8**, page 43 (one per student)

- pens and pencils
- drawing materials
- hole punch

1 Share different encyclopedias with the class. Explain that encyclopedias contain information about a variety of nonfiction topics and are arranged in alphabetical order, much like a dictionary.

2 On the reproducible, students write facts about their topic along with an illustration. Punch holes in each page so they can fit in the looseleaf binder.

3 Arrange finished pages in alphabetical order, punch holes, and put in a classroom binder. Place in the classroom library. As students research more topics, make more reproducibles available to add to the encyclopedia.

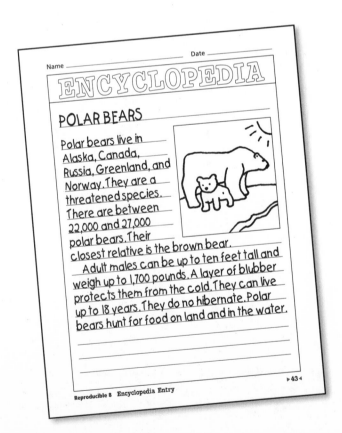

17 Peek-Through Poster

Students present a unique oral report by stepping into the action!

►Materials◄
- butcher paper or posterboard
- drawing supplies
- scissors

1 On a large sheet of butcher paper or posterboard, students draw scenes, maps, or illustrations from their research, leaving holes to poke their heads through. For instance, if a student were researching the old west, he or she may draw a scene of a western town with a hole for a "cowboy's" head to peek through. Or, a student researching the solar system could make his or her head one of the planets!

2 Invite students to present information about their topics while sticking their heads through the holes in their posters. Two students may hold up either side of the poster.

18 Topic Survey

Students conduct a class survey and graph the results.

►Materials◄
- pens and pencils
- paper
- drawing supplies

1 Discuss the variety of topics students are reading about and make a large chart on the board as shown at right.

2 Survey students and put tally marks in the appropriate categories.

Topics	How Many
Historic time period	|||
Animals	╫╫	
Famous people	╫╫ ||
Science	|||

3 Using the information obtained in the survey, and depending on students' levels, they might create their own pie graphs or bar graphs.

19 Where in the World?

Students create a map full of information.

▶Materials◀
- map of the world
- paper
- drawing supplies
- pens and pencils
- pushpins

1 Point out that the research that the students are doing may take them around the world! Display a large world map.

2 Have students cut out a small "flag" (a small rectangular piece of paper).

3 Invite students to write a fact about their topic on their flag and pin it to the appropriate area of the map. For example: *Panda bears live in the bamboo jungles of China. The Gold Rush started in California.*

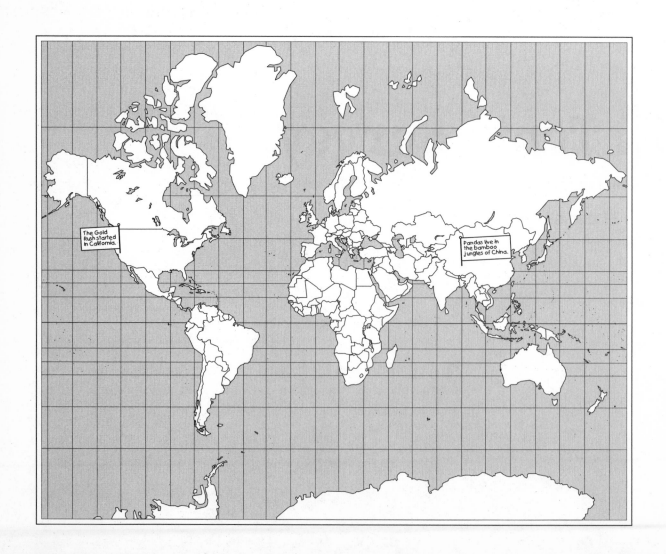

20 Wear It Out!

Students show off their research by wearing it!

►Materials◄

- plain paper grocery bag (one per student)
- scissors
- drawing materials
- pens and pencils
- glue
- found objects

1 Cut out holes for the arms and head as shown in the diagram below. Cut up the middle to make it into a vest.

2 Invite students to write, draw, and decorate their vest with facts and illustrations about their topics. Students might write their topic on the front of the vest along with some questions (the answers could be written on the back of the vest). Students may also use real life objects such as a miniature teddy for Teddy Roosevelt or gold coins for pirates. Students may wear their vests when making a presentation or walk around with them on at a sharing party.

3 Use the extra paper from cutting out the vest to make pockets! Fill the pockets with information cards or found objects related to the topic.

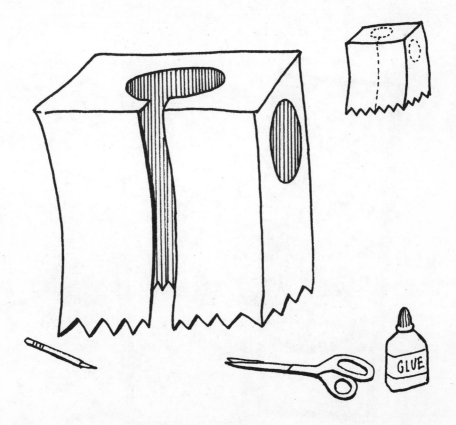

21 Famous Figure Bookmarks

Students make bookmarks to teach others about a topic.

►Materials◄

- construction paper
- drawing supplies
- scissors
- hole punch
- yarn

1 Explain to students that advertisers make promotional materials to sell their products. Tell students that they will be advertising their topics by creating promotional bookmarks.

2 Show students examples of catchy phrases and creative wording in advertisements and have them brainstorm one for their topic.

3 Have students use a ruler to divide a piece of construction paper into four separate rectangular pieces and cut them out. Then have them write a catchy phrase and illustration on one side of the bookmark and information about the topic on the other side.

4 Invite each student to create four different bookmarks about their topics. Upon completion, laminate the bookmarks, hole-punch the tops, and attach a yarn tassel to each one. Place them in books that focus on their topic.

22 Topic TV Game Shows

Students use information about their topics to create a game show.

▶Materials◀

- classroom furniture such as desks, chairs, and bulletin boards
- posterboard
- drawing materials
- pens and pencils
- index cards
- play money
- video camera (optional)

1 Ask students to name some game shows they have seen on TV. Make a list on the board. Ideas might include: *Jeopardy, Wheel of Fortune, Who Wants To Be a Millionaire?,* and *The Price Is Right.*

2 Discuss the rules of each game.

3 Organize students into small groups to create a game show for their topics. Students may use posters, props, illustrations, and flash cards, for authenticity.

4 Pick one group a day (a week) to present their games (with their format of choice), using the class as the contestants and/or audience.

23 Puzzling Topics

Students create puzzles with pictures on front and facts on back.

►Materials◄

- large poster board (one per student)
- scissors
- drawing supplies
- pens and pencils

1 Have students cut the posterboard into nine puzzle pieces.

2 On one side of each puzzle piece, have students write a fact related to their topic. On the flip side, they draw a picture related to the fact.

3 Laminate pieces and place in plastic bags at a center. Students read each piece and then put the puzzle together.

24 Present It in 3-D

Students make a three-dimensional display of a research topic.

►Materials◄

- manila paper (four 14-inch squares per student)
- scissors
- drawing supplies
- stapler

1 Invite students to list four important or interesting facts about their topic. Tell them they'll be illustrating and writing about each fact in a 3-D display.

2 To make the displays, have them fold a manila square in half diagonally to form a triangle. Unfold and fold the opposite corner to form a triangle. Unfold. Cut along one fold line from the corner to the center. Repeat with the remaining manila squares.

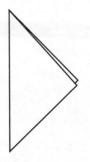
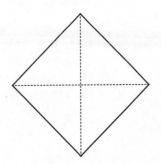

3 Show students how to overlap one triangle made by the cut over the other to form a backdrop that stands on its own, with the overlapped sections as the base. Before stapling, have them decorate and write their fact on the backdrop. Staple through the base. Decorate, fold, and staple the remaining manila squares.

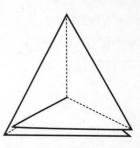

4 Students may arrange their four pieces back to back so that they form a four-section square. Glue together to make a permanent display.

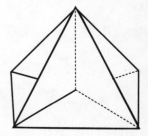

25 Let's Play!

Students create a game based on facts from their research.

►Materials◄

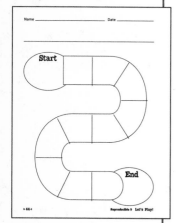

• **reproducible 9**, page 44 (one per student)

• small index cards
• drawing materials
• pens and pencils
• small game pieces
• number cubes

1 Display several board games for students to examine. As a group, make a list of game features on the board. Make another list of the objects of each game.

2 Using the reproducible, have students complete a gameboard that relates to their topic. For example, "Race to the White House," "Find That Koala," or "Journey Through the Universe." Encourage them to think of a title, create rules, and add special steps on the board such as "Get lost in the bamboo jungle! Lose one turn."

3 Have students write questions about their topics on index cards to be used during the game.

4 Students may bring in and decorate shirt boxes to use as containers for their games.

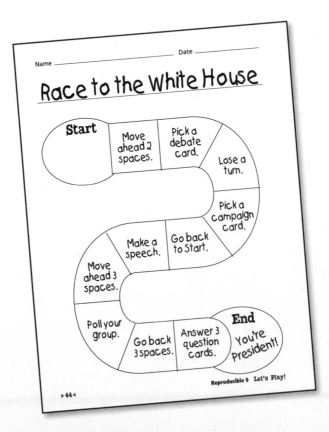

26 Shape Report

Students create a nonfiction picture poem.

►Materials◄

- notebook paper
- white drawing paper
- drawing materials
- pens and pencils

1 Explain to the students that "concrete poetry" is a special type of poetry where the text itself forms a picture on the page.

2 On a blank piece of notebook paper, have students write down five sentences about their research topics. Emphasize that they may be creative with their wording, but the sentences need not rhyme.

3 Distribute blank drawing paper. Invite students to draw lightly, in pencil, the outline of an object that relates to their topic.

4 Students then use this line as a guide to create a poem that takes the shape of its subject. For instance, if the topic is electricity, the poem may take the shape of a light bulb.

27 Testing 1, 2, 3

Students test their classmates' knowledge of different subject areas.

→Materials◄
- lined paper
- pens and pencils

1 Discuss the different types of test questions (true/false, multiple choice, essay, fill in the blank).

2 On a blank sheet of notebook paper, have students write down at least ten facts about their topics.

3 Guide students to change one of their facts into a test question. For example:

Fact: About 490 one-dollar bills make a pound.
Test Question: True or false? It takes more than 400 one-dollar bills to make a pound.

Fact: President Thomas Jefferson asked Lewis and Clark to lead an expedition to the west coast of America.
Test Question: _____ asked Lewis and Clark to lead an expedition to the west coast of America.

4 Have each student create a test with ten questions and an answer key on the back.

5 Laminate tests and place in a center with wipe-off markers. Or, have children trade papers and take each others' tests!

28 Cereal Box Reports

Students decorate cereal boxes with facts and pictures representing their topics.

→Materials←

- empty, clean cereal boxes (one per student)
- white drawing paper
- drawing supplies
- scissors
- glue

1 Have students trace around each of the four upright sides of the box on drawing paper and cut them out.

2 Have students label one large side with the name of their topic. Then have them decorate the remaining sides with illustrations, facts, vocabulary, photos, diagrams, and so on. For example, students may list vocabulary words on one of the thin sides of the box and make a timeline on the other. Students might create a catchy phrase to cover the front of the box along with a colorful picture or drawing. If desired, students may leave the top of the cereal box open to store research information inside the box.

3 Have students glue the decorated sheets to the sides of the cereal box and display.

29 Research Evaluation

Students reflect on their research by filling out an evaluation form.

▶Materials◀

- **reproducible 10**, page 45 (one per student)

- pens and pencils

1 Explain to students that they will be evaluating their research to examine their successes and challenges. By analyzing the research process, students become more aware of how to investigate and explore the world around them. Instruct students to complete the questions on the reproducible.

2 Hold student conferences after reading their evaluations forms to discuss their answers. This may be used as an assessment tool.

30 Research Party

Celebrate and share what you've learned with a party!

At the conclusion of your research unit, have students share what they have learned by hosting a Research Party. Decorate the classroom with all the projects you have created during the unit. Invite other classes, school personnel, and families to the party. Here are some party ideas.

Have students give a speech using their peek-through posters.

Encourage students to dress up in attire matching their subject matter.

Give out door prizes such as bookmarks, toys, and fact cards.

Have students display their work on their desks. As visitors look at the projects, students can answer questions about their topics.

Hold a news conference.

Hand out copies of research-based math word problems for visitors to solve.

Invite visitors to play research-based games.

_____

_____

_____
Date

Dear _____ ,

_____

_____

_____

_____

_____

_____

_____

_____

_____

_____

_____

_____
Name

30 Nonfiction Book Reports   Scholastic Professional Books

Reproducible 1   Facts in the Mail

Name _____ Date _____

TIMES

_____

[image box]

_____

_____
_____
_____
_____
_____

_____

_____

_____   [image box]

_____

_____

_____

_____

Name _____ Date _____

30 Nonfiction Book Reports   Scholastic Professional Books

Reproducible 3   Magazine Cover

Fun Fact Card

Topic _____

Fun Facts

Card created by _____

_____

Topic _____

Name _____ Date _____

Catalog Name _____

_____

_____

_____

_____

_____

_____

_____

_____

_____

_____

_____

_____

_____

_____

_____

_____

_____

_____

_____

_____

_____

_____

_____

_____

_____

_____

_____

_____

30 Nonfiction Book Reports   Scholastic Professional Books

Reproducible 5   Made to Order

Topic 2

Topic 1

Reproducible 6   Compare It!

My Topic

by

Reproducible 7   Documentary

Name _____ Date _____

ENCYCLOPEDIA

_____

_____

_____

_____

_____

_____

_____

_____

_____

_____

_____

_____

_____

_____

_____

30 Nonfiction Book Reports Scholastic Professional Books

Name _____ Date _____

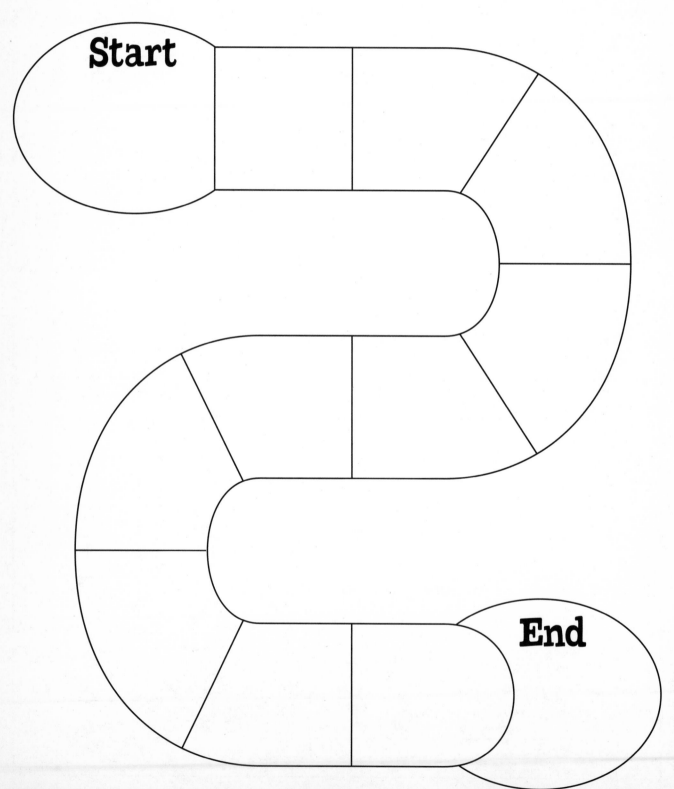

Reproducible 9   Let's Play!

Research Evaluation

Topic: _____

1. Why did you chose this topic? _____

_____

2. What resources did you use? _____

_____

3. What was the most interesting thing you learned? _____

_____

_____

4. What was the most surprising thing you learned? _____

_____

_____

5. What was the hardest part of doing your research? _____

_____

_____

6. Would you read more about your topic? _____

_____

Before my research:
I thought nonfiction was

_____

After my research:
I think nonfiction is

_____

Bibliography of Children's Nonfiction

Nonfiction Series

Eyewitness Books

Ancient Rome by Simon James (Dorling Kindersley, 1990)

Money by Joe Cribb (Dorling Kindersley, 1990)

Volcano and Earthquakes by Susanna Van Rose (Dorling Kindersley, 1992)

If You Lived... series

If You Lived at the Time of Martin Luther King, Jr. by Ellen Levine (Scholastic, 1994)

If You Lived at the Time of the Civil War by Kay Moore (Scholastic, 1994)

If You Lived in Colonial Times by Ann McGovern (Scholastic, 1992)

Scholastic Encyclopedia of...

Animals by Laurence P. Pringle (Scholastic, 2001)

How Things Work by Claire Llewelyn (Scholastic, 2000)

Presidents and Their Times by David Rubel (Scholastic, 2001)

Women in the United States by Sheila Keenan (Scholastic, 1996)

Magic Tree House Research Guides (Random House)

Dinosaurs by Will Osborne and Mary Pope Osborne (Random House, 2000)

Knights and Castles by Will Osborne and Mary Pope Osborne (Random House, 2000)

Mummies and Pyramids by Will Osborne and Mary Pope Osborne (Random House, 2001)

Rain Forests by Will Osborne and Mary Pope Osborne (Random House, 2001)

Space by Will Osborne and Mary Pope Osborne (Random House, 2002)

Step-Up Biographies (Random House)

Meet Abraham Lincoln by Barbara Cary (Random House, 1989)

Meet George Washington by Joan Heilbroner (Random House, 1989)

Hello Readers (Scholastic)

A Boy Named Boomer by Boomer Esiason (Scholastic, 1995)

A Girl Named Helen Keller by Margo Lundell (Scholastic, 1995)

Rookie Biography (Children's Press)

Elizabeth Blackwell: First Woman Doctor by Carol Greene (1991)

Madam C. J. Walker: Pioneer Businesswoman by Marlene Toby (1995)

Margaret Wise Brown by Carol Greene (1994)

Childhoods of Famous Americans (Aladdin)

Clara Barton, Founder of the American Red Cross by Augusta Stevenson (Aladdin, 1986)

Henry Ford: Young Man With Ideas by Hazel B. Aird (Aladdin, 1986)

Roberto Clemente: Young Ball Player by Montrew Dunham (Aladdin, 1997)

Sitting Bull: Dakota Boy by Augusta Stevenson (Aladdin, 1996)

Troll Biographies (Troll Publishing)

Young Martin Luther King, Jr.: I Have a Dream by Joanne Mattern (Troll, 1991)

Young Rosa Parks: A Civil Rights Heroine by Anne Benjamin (Troll, 1996)

Women of Our Times (Puffin)

Laura Ingalls Wilder: Growing Up in the Little House by Patricia Reilly Giff (Puffin, 1996)

Mary McLeod Bethune: Voice of Black Hope by Milton Meltzer (Puffin, 1996)

Our Golda: The Story of Golda Meir by David A. Adler (Puffin, 1986)

David Adler's Picture Books

A Picture Book of Fredrick Douglass by David Adler (Chelsea House, 1995)

A Picture Book of Helen Keller by David Adler (Chelsea House, 1992)

A Picture Book of John F. Kennedy by David Adler (Chelsea House, 1999)

A Picture Book of Paul Revere by David Adler (Chelsea House, 1995)

A Picture Book of Simon Bolivar by David Adler (Chelsea House, 1992)

Gateway Biographies (Millbrook Publishing)

Bill Clinton: President of the 90s by Robert Cwiklik (Millbrook, 1997)

Bill Gates: Computer King by Josepha Sherman (Millbrook, 2000)

Colin Powell: Straight to the Top by Rose Blue (Millbrook, 1997)

Lives of... (Harcourt Brace)

Lives of the Artists: Masterpieces, Messes (And What the Neighbors Thought) by Kathleen Krull (Harcourt, 1995)

Lives of the Athletes: Thrills, Spills (And What the Neighbors Thought) by Kathleen Krull (Harcourt, 1999)

Lives of the Musicians: Good Times, Bad Times (And What the Neighbors Thought) by Kathleen Krull (Harcourt, 1993)

Lives of the Presidents by Kathleen Krull (Harcourt, 1998)

Lives of the Writers: Comedies, Tragedies (And What the Neighbors Thought) by Kathleen Krull (Harcourt, 1994)

Science/Nature

A Drop of Water by Walter Wick (Scholastic, 1997)

The Extinct Alphabet Book by Jerry Pallotta (Charlesbridge, 1993)

Monarchs by Kathyrn Lasky (Harcourt Brace, 1993)

The Pumpkin Book by Gail Gibbons (Holiday House, 1999)

Tornado by Stephen Kramer (Carolrhoda, 1992)

Wolves by Seymour Simon (Harper Collins, 1993)

Math

Ben Franklin and the Magic Squares (Random House, 2001)

Count Your Way Through China by Jim Haskins (Carolrhoda, 1988)

The Go-Around Dollar by Barbara Johnston Adams (Four Winds Press, 1992)

Math for Fun: Exploring Numbers by Andrew King (Copper Beech Books, 1998)

Mission Addition by Loreen Leedy (Holiday House, 1997)

Subtraction Action by Loreen Leedy (Holiday House, 2000)

Social Studies

By the Dawn's Early Light: The Story of the Star Spangled Banner by Stephen Kroll (Scholastic, 1994)

The Century for Young People by Peter Jennings and Todd Brewster (Doubleday, 1999)

The Great Fire by Jim Murphy (Scholastic, 1995)

Exploring the Titanic by Robert Ballard (Scholastic, 1988)

Immigrant Kids by Russell Freedman (Scholastic, 1980)

Shhh...We're Writing the Constitution by Jean Fritz (Putnam, 1983)

Notable Picture Books with Biographical Subject

Amelia and Eleanor Go For a Ride: Based on a True Story by Pam Munoz Ryan (Scholastic, 1999)

America's Champion Swimmer by David Adler (Raintree/Steck-Vaughn, 2000)

The Babe and I by David Adler (Gulliver, 1999)

Cleopatra by Diane Stanley (William Morrow, 1994)

The Legend of the Teddy Bear by Frank Murphy (Sleeping Bear, 2000)

Leonardo Da Vinci by Diane Stanley (William Morrow, 1996)

Lou Gehrig: The Luckiest Man by David Adler (Gulliver, 1997)

Pioneer Girl: The Story of Laura Ingalls Wilder by William Anderson (HarperCollins, 1998)

Snowflake Bentley by Jacqueline Briggs Martin (Houghton Mifflin, 1998)

The Starry Messenger by Peter Sis (Farrar Straus & Giroux, 1996)

Steamboat! The Story of Captain Blanche Leathers by Judith Heide Gilliland (Dorling Kindersley, 2000)

Stone Girl, Bone Girl: the Story of Mary Anning by Laurence Anholt (Orchard, 1999)

Tutankhamen's Gift by Robert Sabuda (Atheneum, 1994)

What's the Big Idea, Ben Franklin? by Jean Fritz (Putnam, 1976)

William Shakespeare and the Globe by Aliki (HarperCollins, 2000)

Wilma Unlimited: How Wilma Rudolph Became the World's Fastest Woman by Kathleen Krull (Harcourt Brace, 1996)

You Forgot Your Skirt, Amelia Bloomer by Shana Corey (Scholastic, 2000)

Young Teddy Roosevelt by Cheryll Harness (National Geographic Society, 1998)

Computer Connections

The following are helpful web sites for information on biographies. Teacher guidance is suggested in order to ensure appropriate web site content.

http://www.yahooligans.com/ This kid safe search engine is a web guide that includes a dictionary, encyclopedia, reference tools, games and access to topics such as around the world, science/nature, and school subjects.

http://sunsite.berkeley.edu/KidsClick!/ This is a websearch for kids by librarians and includes such subjects as: facts and reference, science and math, the arts, machines and transportation, society and government, and more.

http://www.ajkids.com/ This is the kids version of the web search engine called Ask Jeeves. Students can type in a question and ajkids will confirm the question being asked and then look for websites that can answer that question.

http://www.awesomelibrary.org/ This site is a library that contains more than 5,000 web sites to search for information. Topics include: social studies, math, science, English, and special topics such as the Olympics and the environment.

http://www.americaslibrary.gov This web site is sponsored by the Library of Congress and offers entertaining facts and stories about American history.

Magazines

Cobblestone (Cobblestone Publishing)

Muse (Carus Publishing)

Ranger Rick (National Wildlife Federation)

Scholastic News (Scholastic)

Smithsonian (The Smithsonian Institute)

Sports Illustrated for Kids (Time Inc.)

Super Science (Scholastic)

Time for Kids (Time Inc.)

3-2-1 Contact (Children's Television Workshop)